My Visit to the Doctor

Rachel Tisdale

Photography by Chris Fairclough

W
FRANKLIN WATTS
LONDON•SYDNEY

First published in 2007 by
Franklin Watts
338 Euston Road
London NW1 3BH

Franklin Watts Australia
Level 17/207 Kent Street
Sydney NSW 2000

ISBN: 978 0 7496 7455 7 (hbk)
ISBN: 978 0 7496 7467 0 (pbk)

Dewey classification number: 610.69

WORCESTERSHIRE COUNTY COUNCIL		
	985	
Bertrams		19.10.07
J610.69		£8.99
WS		

A CIP catalogue record for this book is available from the British Library.

Planning and production by Discovery Books Limited
Editor: James Nixon
Designer: Ian Winton
Photography: Chris Fairclough
Series advisors: Diana Bentley MA and Dee Reid MA,
Fellows of Oxford Brookes University

The author, packager and publisher would like to thank the following people for their participation in this book: Arran and Kam Bola, Diane Payne and the staff at Quinborne Medical Practice.

All photographs by Chris Fairclough.

Printed in China

Franklin Watts is a division of Hachette Children's books, an Hachette Livre UK company.

Contents

Feeling unwell

Arran has earache.
He has to visit the
doctor.

Mum makes an appointment.

The surgery

Mum and Arran arrive at the surgery.

The waiting room

Arran waits to see the doctor.

The doctor rings the bell.

You can go in now.

The doctor

11

Ear infection

The doctor looks
inside Arran's ear.

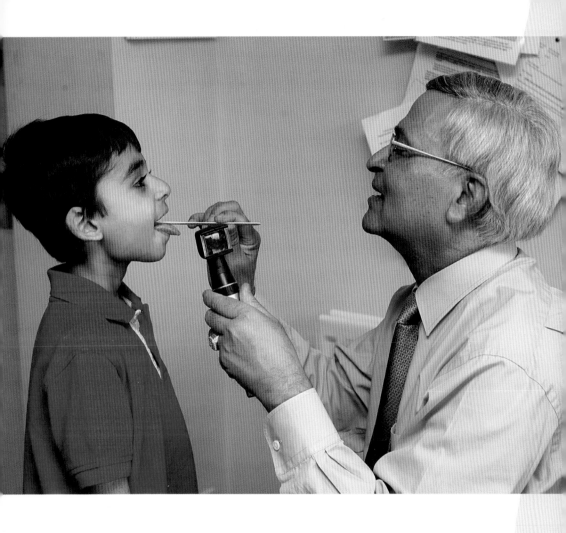

Then he checks
Arran's throat.

A prescription

Arran needs some medicine. The doctor prints a prescription.

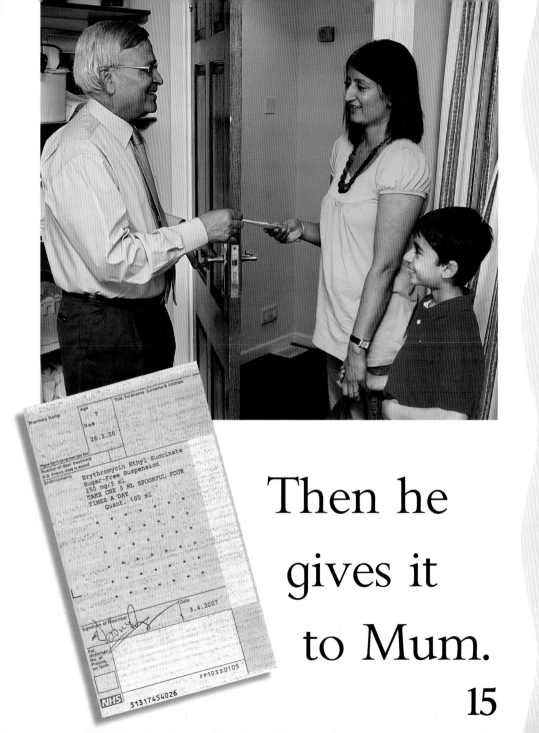

Then he
gives it
to Mum.

15

Leaving the surgery

Mum and Arran leave the surgery.

17

The pharmacy

Mum and Arran go to the pharmacy to get Arran's medicine.

Mum gives the prescription to the assistant.

You must sign it here.

Medicine

The chemist finds the right medicine for Arran.

Feeling better

Arran takes his medicine every day.

Soon he feels much better.

23

Word bank

Look back for these words and pictures.

Assistant

Chemist

Doctor

Earache

Medicine

Pharmacy

Prescription

Surgery

Waiting room